€8

THE USES OF SILK

Gráinne Tobin

THE USES OF SILK

ARLEN
HOUSE

The Uses of Silk

is published in 2018 by
ARLEN HOUSE
42 Grange Abbey Road
Baldoyle, Dublin 13, Ireland
Phone: 00 353 86 8360236
arlenhouse@gmail.com
arlenhouse.blogspot.com

Distributed internationally by
SYRACUSE UNIVERSITY PRESS
621 Skytop Road, Suite 110
Syracuse, NY 13244–5290
Phone: 315–443–5534
Fax: 315–443–5545
supress@syr.edu
syracuseuniversitypress.syr.edu

ISBN 978–1–85132–195–7, paperback

Typesetting by Arlen House

cover image: 'Ballykinlar Looking Across Dundrum Bay' by
Jim Manley is reproduced courtesy of the artist

CONTENTS

for Siún and Danny Carden

THE USES OF SILK

WHERE WERE YOU IN 1916?
– Brendan Behan, *The Hostage*

I wasn't born. Excuses, always excuses!
Of course I wasn't born, but I was present
with a quarter of the country's population
at the Eucharistic Congress of 1932,
latent in a pair of ten-year-olds who were yet to meet.

An ovum in her reserves, the boast of Catholic Ireland,
I hid inside my mother, wearing her good coat
on the excursion train from Portarlington
in fine weather, said to be God's answer
to thirty-seven-thousand spiritual acts of self-denial
undertaken by the new and ancient nation
and placed on record in the archbishop's office.

The child who grew up to be my father
wore the lanyard and badges of a Limerick troop
of the Catholic Boy Scouts of Ireland,
one of fourteen hundred plucky little fellows
encamped with trench latrines on a boarding-school lawn
and tireless in fifteen acres of the Phoenix Park,
directing a million pilgrims, holding lines and fetching water.

Where are their two faces in the crowd
that knelt with its shriven leaders in the grass?
The hungry streets, a supernatural toyshop
of angelic toy theatres, as by night
the Post Office roof beamed sky-writing,
GLORIFICAMUS. And I hear the last
of the ornate urinals made for the Congress
was bought in the seventies by a student of art.

Fons et Origo, 1940

Dear Little Brother Brendan –
I'm learning Spanish at college. I can say
my hands are in the pockets of my trousers
so I'm all set to impress the *senoritas*.
I got Mammy the two dozen fine wool vests,
standing poker faced among the ladies' frillies
below in Clerys' sale, with a queue behind me,
and it all pulled out on the counter for me to pick.
Yes, I'll send you my camel-hair coat for the dance,
on the Limerick train in this week's suitcase
with the twenty-four vests and my dirty washing.
But don't be complaining it's too long for you,
and don't let you-know-who get beer on it.
I saw a girl walk into a lecture
with her books under her arm.
Mick's sister says she's from the Bog of Allen
and known as a brain, but she thinks I am brash.
I hear she goes to the dairy some mornings
for a glass of fresh milk and a bun,
and Brendan, I'm going to be there.

CONJOINED

In those days I had four hands, eight limbs,
four kidneys, two hearts that beat as one, etcetera –
my mother's internal Siamese twin,
ready to detach in the fullness, etcetera.

I must have sucked the smaller of our two left thumbs
in utero but, as this was 1951,
I have no scans to prove it, no foetal photographs
while I quickened, rolled and squirmed,
unclenched my fists, dunted her belly,
bounced soap into her bathwater.

Was I dreaming in my amniotic pool
inside my fleshly diving bell? She said she dreamt of me,
linked by my diver's tube to everything she sent,
her blood and breath, her air and shore,
sharing her inwardness while she prayed
to be increased, to be able for all of it,
then gave up asking the mother of Christ for help
in the mysterious ordeal of our separation,
once she'd been told the baby god was born
by a miracle that left his virgin mother
knowing nothing about it, unsullied and unbirthed,
intact as all the men in charge could wish,
in 1951. Etcetera.

LEARNING TO WHISTLE

At four years old you don't yet know enough
to give up learning what you need to learn.

Your soft mouth practices the O of kissing,
the puff to put out candles on a cake,

thousands of repetitions. You're in training.
The big ones ridicule your straining face,

neighbours insist you'll make Our Lady cry,
rhyme off whistling women, crowing hens,

but your daddy says don't mind them, try again,
no attempt is false. Draw in your lips,

flatten your tongue behind milk teeth,
believing that the tune belongs to you,

and clear your palate for the rolling breath
to find the moment when your note comes true.

SOILED

Books came from the County Library
in raw wood trunks the size to hide a child,
greased with use and readers' sweat.
Two big girls lugged them in,
gripping their sea-chest handles.

Our gummed-paper collage filled the classroom wall,
followed the four seasons in torn-off shreds of colour
we all got turns to lick and stick together.

Weeks rolled over us. Winter was dangerous
with afternoon twilights which our teacher said
meant the end of the world, the three dark days foretold.

Miss lived with her sister in a redbrick terrace.
Striped canvas kept their polished door
from sunlight and the heat of summer.

The teacher's big oak desk was topped
by sugar paper stuck with Sellotape
to shield the wood from dirty copybooks.

A rota of girls disinfected the doorknob
to kill the germs our fingers brought
from playground and toilets
and our filthy homes and daisy chains
we spent May and June constructing in the grass
which grew outdoors in unhygienic soil.

BUYING KNICKERS WITH AUNTIE MAUREEN

Soon after the moon landing and during the Vatican Council,
but before I get my first bra,
in a front-room draper's in Skerries, County Dublin,
my Auntie Maureen asks to see some knickers.

A bored young priestess or curator searches
the archive shelves, holds up a sample pair
that might fit snugly on one of my aunt's kneecaps.

Maureen forbears to speak but raises eyebrows,
her expression like an Easter Island ancestor.
The face is saying: *I am buying knickers*
for an abdomen that has housed thirteen babies,
of whom nine lived. I am Hecuba, Brigid, Maeve.

The girl delves in her cabinet, brings out a garment
for a goddess, a queen of the fuller figure,
and slowly, Maureen nods at flowered cotton,
laid out like a treaty for signature.

A girl in black brings in more spuds, *ta-dah!*
Loudspeaker music fades, as mute air drops
around our shoulders, and the post-Mass lunch crowd
stops talking in the echo of my shouted explanation
– or my old, lip-reading father's question –
so what did this priest do, exactly?

I'm floating in a soundproof zorbing ball
as my father bobs past in his sealed transparent orb,
in a sea full of synchronised swimmers
wearing flowered bathing caps and lipstick –
I lift a mike and try to speak, miming
for him to put his earphones on, but the volume
is not enough, so I get out the notebook
and thick felt-tip to answer in black headlines.

At every table the diners are chatting again,
unable not to know more than any of us can bear
of what this Father did to boys in the seaside cottage,
though today's sermon left out that bit,
while my deaf dad drifts by, shaking his head,
mentioning them already in his prayers.

Upon a time, at a funfair made by artists,
we went inside a balloon as big as a house,
with stretchy rubber walls that muffled sound
and held us safe as we fell and boinged between them,
a womby tent for playing Jonah's whale.
I've a photo of my father with my children,
bouncing slowly through the branching corridors
of this Eggopolis, in blue subaqueous light.

THE BULL MONAGHAN CLIP

If my father were to visit as a revenant
we would sit together on the garden love seat
I shanghaied him into buying for his smoking,
    foothering with matches,
    cupping the bowl of his pipe
against the wind
as the flame took his phantom puff,
    enlivening the pressed leaves within
    for what pleasure was left.

I'd say, tell me again
how you learned to make the movements of the alphabet
    with your finger
    in a shallow tray of sand
so that to the end
    your letters were worth having
and tell me about your teachers at the Brothers.

 Footage projected in a beam of pipe smoke,
    cinéma verité scenes,
    low-angled jump-cuts.

Brother Young –
we always called him Cricky –
he called me Walther,
    I don't know why –
and the Bull Monaghan –
    he was a big man, and he roared!

Close-ups of round towers
    drawn on the covers
    of children's copybooks
in the young Free State.

The Bull pawing the floor
　　by the chalky blackboard,
darkening air over boys
　　in home-knit sweaters –
his champion's shoulders
　　and his snorting rages,
bulking up
　　among scratched desks and inkwells –
his wounded bull's head,
　　and the smell of the cloth off him.

MEMORANDUM

A young man brought in bread and salt
when floors and walls were new and bare,
set coal in corners of the house,
prayed for the family's food and fire.

Children were born in that back room,
particles from skin and breath
drifting out into her garden,
settling in our mother's tilth.

The urge to use things up increases
as things to use increase in cupboards –
keeping the stuff of lives for spares,
making do, making amends.

And now this page from the scrap paper box
turns out not to be blank at all,
saved from a half-used copybook
but still not quite disposable.

Iris stylosa, phlox pan, saxifraga fortunei:
a relic from her planting notes,
her biro sprung against the line –
flowers she introduced by name
when soul and senses still kept time.

He always bought too much. The multipacks
of Bo-Peep matches, Imperial Leather soap,
twelve dozen – a gross – one hundred and forty four
packets of Erin dried potato soup
stacked up against another famine,
or pressed on offspring heading out the door
to jobs and universities, his message shaken
among the dehydrated flakes, for nobody
said out loud the words 'I love you' then,
and even though he's five years buried,
his store well past its best by date,
our seven kitchens are supplied
with an inheritance of soup and matches,
perfumed soap still in its cellophane,
in case the day comes when we'll need
to be provided for, or to provide.

A Shrine to the Ancestors

In place of a red candle bulb
before a picture of the Sacred Heart,
we venerate found objects
in a sealed reliquary
of stinkproof glass.

His last filled pipe
of burnt-out Mick McQuaid.

Her folk art matchbox
from the coach trip
to the tulip fields.

His Maguire and Paterson's
Bo-Peep safety matches
in an illustrated box
showing a ruined castle
against a brave blue sky.

Her twenty ladylike Silk Cut
elegant in white but for the words
in their black border.

Smoking seriously harms you
and others around you.

FEW TREES HAVE BEEN HARMED IN THE MAKING
OF THIS POEM
after Siobhán Hapaska

Strictly speaking I'm dead,
torn out of the soil
that kept me going.

Laid out, waked,
in a clear white space,
held horizontal by thin cables
of polished steel.

Beaded olives hang from my branches.
I have been made an airborne
image of myself.

My fallen leaves, my web of dusty roots
are carefully displayed.
Nothing's wasted, nothing living dies,
nothing is created or destroyed.

I am modest as a dancing bride,
fruitful as a matriarch.
I hold it all in balance.
There is life after me.

NOTE
for Lila Stuart

Everything with me is on the back boiler,
and the arse is out of every saucepan in the house.

A magic stockpot full of onion, carrot peelings,
herb stalks and the dodgy bits of leeks,
the skin and bone of passing days, topped up
as and when, detritus not to be discarded –
gathering strength on the back of the hob,
while ordinary hours shout for attention
and the elixir concentrates to danger point.

If you don't do something soon, you'll find
the kitchen filled with fumes that sting your eyes,
stop up your mouth and catch at the back of your throat,
the delicious makings boiled to toxic varnish,
your heaviest pan a crucible of loss.

BULLDOG CLIPS

Paired off in the packet, they do that thing
you see in films, the open-mouthed big kiss
of lovers kicking shut the door behind them,
locked together so you're not supposed to think
of the seventeen people – directors, gaffers and grips,
the cameras, boom, sets and props –
around at this intimate moment,
making a show of these two left alone
with their personal magnetism, attracted,
nay, clipped-on to each other, until one
breaks the seal, and their mouths in profile,
in soft-lit close-up, part, gasp, gulp,
a little fish-like, a little bit Nemo,
grabbing the beloved's upper lip
between their two, opening and closing
as if they're chewing, swallowing air,
a pincer action that brings to mind
telltale twelve-year-olds at the junior disco –
Miss! They're eating the face off each other!

The Decorum of the Social Wasp

Wasps prefer to be left alone to get on with it,
are despised but mannerly and not hysterical,
unlike the peacock butterflies, easy, metaphorical,
posing on buddleia, cushions and crockery,
unwrapping themselves like debutantes,
lighting on your open page, or on your face,
unsteady drunks, too sure of their welcome.

If silvery streaks appear like greying hair
in the auburn grain of your garden table,
sit and admire the pewter sheen uncovered,
avoiding online forums of mass slaughter,
tips for poison, burning, boiling water,
and even if you catch the queen of wasps
in the discreet act of eating furniture,
allow her to return, a tiny monster,
to chew the pulp to make her teardrop nest.

FROGMATES AT WHATSTANDWELL

Three beanbag frogs, stacked back-to-back
among the settled trinkets on our shelf,
hug each other in the same stunned attitude
as the live frogs mustering one afternoon
in a dead-end backwater of the Derwent,
heavy with leaves and insect hum
near our trailer trash starter-home:
the frog-filled surface rippling only slightly
from the skinny males' gymnastic leaps
onto bulging females, who mostly kick them
back into the water, though all the frogs
look drugged, stupefied, or in a stoic trance,
a languid orgy, a gently-seething mass,
males jumping, floppy as thrown beanbags,
on top of mated pairs inertly locked together,
latecomers dithering like drunks,
clutching any frog they can till shaken off
into the water, as if frogs feel the lack
of kisses – princely suitors
yearning for release.

ODE TO THE RED SQUIRRELS OF TOLLYMORE FOREST

Come on you reds, you dancers! *Sciurus vulgaris*
– what a cheek to call them common.

There should be more, but life gets in their way,
pine cones chewed to stalks, nut-stores forgotten,
grey pox that melts their faces and then kills them,
for all the germinating hoards they leave behind them,
their kittenish leaps, their chuck chuck tutting,
their chirrup, their buzz, their scratch and sniffing.

And when I asked him what he thought
of the simile for orgasm proposed
by a daft girl in a sitcom, my man said
no, not so much like fairies on tiny motorcycles
whizzing round a wall of death,
but more like red squirrels zooming up tree trunks
into the larch canopy of Tollymore Forest –
a *ratatat* ginger burst that stops you right there,
knocks you backwards, looking round to catch
that dazzle where it sparks to eagle height,
branching to cross eyed infinity and down again,
poised in its own speed like some particle in physics
that is a wave and isn't, and fools you every time.

Some Kind of Nature Poem

Cursing the dog shit and the dogs, cursing the owners
who insist their beastly turds are so organic,
biodegradable even, that there's no need
for the poop scoop and the plastic bag,
I'm watching the path my feet are on
when a blue-green pulsating handball,
varnished glassy and unnatural,
bursts open at my approach
into a swarm of green-bottle blowflies
on half a furred grey pygmy shrew,

and then, at the clearing where the sea
suddenly breathes, and a bower of pines
makes a proscenium arch
backlit with afternoon sky,
I meet the eye of another,
a fallow deer, a doe, standing still,
staring at me as I stare back at her,
both of us quiet, holding our ground,
until she darts her head, skitters up into the forest,
and, as I turn for home, my boots find easy footing,
I hear the tree trunks creaking
right through to the soles of my feet.

GULLED

Big swivel-headed lumps of rudeness,
herring gulls stand splat-footed on the table
of the café where we drink glasses of mint tea
inside castle walls, high up above the beach
and landmarks of a southern town.

Their whitish under-feathers appear stained
as if they rub them into urine-puddled corners,
and their hooky yellow beaks have a red spot
for focusing when looking down their noses
out of their red-rimmed yellow eyes
like vulgar autocrats, demanding all they want
on principle, because they can.

Grey backs, black wingtips, pink stalky feet –
they caw, whinge, quack and howl in air,
laments and protests, an urgent utterance
I'm not prepared to entertain.
But their ancestors were wheeling wide
round these battlements when the Moors
set stone on top of stone.
These birds lack charm – their flesh and feather,
gristle and keratin have not evolved
to make a human want a cuddle.

They live on the lookout, one jaundiced eye
on the main chance, and the other, unblinking,
in the opposite direction, checking out
the interesting, the edible,
unafraid of us and our proprieties.

In flight they are forgiven, riding the airspace
with feet tucked smooth as ballet dancers,
tipping and whirling at their ease, and ours,
as long as they stay far enough away.

Feedback at the Seafood Bar

They call me madam here and I don't mind.
I'm a late visitor and camouflaged.
Voices gather overhead
like a racket of fieldfares flocking
to feed on a bush of bright berries.
The waiter arrives, holding up my plate,
an altarboy swinging a censer,
drifting the smell of roasted rosemary,
and an American migrant perched beside me
stops her alarm call with a look of pleasure,
chirrups *it's nice here* in a dress the green
of parakeets' wings, as they split the bill.
Her native companion warbles in harmony,
and blessedly, nobody notices me.

In Praise of the Water Treatment Plant
at Newcastle Harbour

The roofs and roads are black with rain
and the sea pocked with it   until the sky
swoons and dissolves into another grey

but look there   by the yellow marker buoy
a pale parabola of a different glaze
an obstacle   a wake   that the sea flows round
a spreading ellipse   parallel to land
its sliding surface scratched by ragged jets
boiling up from the outflow pipe below
into the sleek blue grey   flecked by white terns
bouncing underwater   and back to the world of air

hunting the little fish whirled to their gape
by the sewage works it took all year to build

last winter's tides   topping its concrete cliffs
drenching monster pumps   and tiny men
the town's floods bursting in from every drain

but the drowned green roof grew fresh with blow-ins
and these wet days the water's clear
down to the dark-washed kelp and seabed stones.

A Sympathy Visit from Madame Alfred Carrière

In this grim November, or *Brumaire*,
when nobody can bear to know the news,
among the wind-browned leaves white roses bloom,
casting their scent out to the cold and damp –
persistent, lovely, female, overblown.

The rose bush started with a four-inch slip
cut years ago, and now it tops the hedge,
canoodles with the telegraph pole on the corner,
where a green path climbs the slope between the houses
to our lackadaisical street above the harbour.

The rose is Madame Alfred Carrière.
I see her as a powdered Renoir woman
ruffled in chiffon, in her middle years,
murmuring of better times to come –
her perfumed kiss, her smile, my angry tears.

IN A GLASS HOUSE
The Tropical Ravine, Botanic Gardens, Belfast

This gangway
where your footsteps sound
    is your panopticon
you must keep vigil

    glass furred and fogged
in steam bath dankness
    all beyond
blotted and blurred

    sweetheart ferns
spread and cling
    to soaking brickwork
mossy sills

    the drip the tap
the run of moisture
    liquid percussion
creaking branches

    released from bedsits
parlour palms
    and castor oil plants
swell to giants

    in hanging baskets
succulent antlers
    trail from insect-
fretted sconces

    drowsing festoons
of pitcher-plants
    penis gourds
Aladdin's lamps

do not pinch out
the withered shoots
  or steal camellias
for slip or blossom

  try not to cross
the species barrier
  rubbing your cheek
on leaves of striped velvet

  you may be tempted
to court oblivion
  under white blooms
of angels' trumpets

  no throwing coins
into the pond
  in the garden
of life and death.

Here, around the whirlpool of Partition,
when engineering was godliness,
and the doctrine of the city was the purity of its water,
they walled the heather slopes with granite blocks,
trimmed the plughole of the reservoir
in protestant-looking burnt-blue brick,
smoothed to the curve of a brass band horn,
a vortex fed by reeling mountain streams.

Now we tread new tarmac to the bellmouth
– time a spillaway that swallows all –
above the hollow where the workers lived
with Bignian in front and Pov-rty behind,
spelt out in scree on the slope of Pig Mountain.

Here's glinting granite, laid on puddled clay
by giants whose folktale graves lie deep
in boulder fields, who drank their tea
from sooty cans, ate their cold hard porridge sliced,
worked the hills for a boss with a voice like rifle fire.

I smell blood, one said, stopped halfway
in the overflow tunnel before the hooter
sounded a fatal fall. Stone men
– who wore starched shirts to dances
in the recreation hall, watched Chaplin
at the valley picture house – full-grown men,
who'd give a push up to schoolgirls
climbing the Mourne Wall in polished shoes,
dropping down to leave the mountain roughness
to walk the road to Mass in Attical –

girls of twelve who fastened wood shavings
as ringlets in their hair,
whose uncle, one quiet Sunday,

lowered them from the derrick
down the hole half-dug for the dam,
standing in a metal bucket, up to their necks,
to look out on a hundred feet of dark,
at grit and water leaking between cast-iron plates
that lined the trench and held the walls apart.

THE LADIES' TOILET OF THE IMAGINATION

Let us descend into the underworld
of an invisible toilet between Belfast City Hall
and Robinson and Cleavers' latest window –
under the tarmac where traffic lanes divide,
car tyres spin above the ghostly ceilings
of a Victorian municipal public convenience
for ladies with pennies to spend
on porcelain, mahogany and polished brass,
a subterranean refuge, until deleted
from the streetscape, moved
to the archaeological record,
when mixtape cassettes held incendiaries
and handbags were searched in every shop.

Even if they smashed the tiles and bevelled glass,
tore up copper piping, broke up cisterns,
tipped in lorry loads of quarried roadstone,
poured concrete down the polished stairs,
I would know it was still there,
I would dream of going down those steps
with a coin ready for the heavy door,
some conversation for the other woman
combing her hair at the basin next to mine,
our eyes meeting in the mirror, deciding
neither of us is willing to kill the other.

JUNCTION BOX
Lower Crescent, Belfast

Something is singing
among cracked-up flagstones
under the young leaves
of a lime tree where the park's square edges
nudge the railings of a sooty church,
grey rubblestone still smudged
from the city's smoking past,
            and there it is,
shoulder high, an arm span wide, a big black box
in painted steel with a rutted crust,
the under paper from posters that you can't pick off,
stained and overlapped so in the end
it looks deliberate, distressed graffiti chic,
or like an artwork by Tápies that marks the times
in dirty layers,
            and this is where
it's coming from – the sound –
a sitar-accordion drone,
an old song echoing, an imperfect note,
single yet multiple, voices plaited together
in a chord with no pause, chanting day and night
beside the parking meter and the litter bin.

Using your bus card when the day is auspicious
you can view estates of starter homes
    gaps of reedy bogland
      poor grazing
          applications pending
little messes of gravel and garbage
    run-off streaming in its channel
        into the disused reservoir bordered in cement
fuzzy-felt grass banks
    model earthworks
      a clachan of brick-paper sheds
tidy waves bumped by the wind
    as if blown through a drinking straw
and set to pause on glittering water
    one mute swan.

Though you twist on your Translink plush
    the *aisling* will vanish at the forty limit
your vision fill with rusted crates
    blown litter at the backs of factories
      accident repair signs
        furniture showrooms
deserted offices stacked full of papers
    the cemetery bus shelter
      handy for the shops.

ABSENT

Vase or woman, the optical illusion
swings back and forth from both to neither
– what used to be there, what is there now.

The passenger giving directions to his childhood home
tells the driver to turn left where the post office was,
but now it's a roundabout on a suburban bypass,
embedded in fifty miles of commuters' tarmac.

A time comes when everything you see
is double exposed, the mile you walked on Sundays
between hedges of May blossom
overprinted with steel fences and For Sale signs
where the developer packed up and left.

PASSING NUMBER TWENTY
Ballynahinch

Among fake frontages on derelict shops, someone
with money and sense has handed us a share
in this defiance – granite doorstep, polished brass –
has hung curtains of fine lace to shade an aspidistra
which may not exist beyond the long front windows.
Is it a folly, to put hope in good repair?

Two tall storeys, glossy with sage-green paint,
though grass sprouts in nearby gutters, and wages
have drained away. The courtyard's double doors
are latched wide open, now there are no more horses
to be stabled in these streets, no servant girls,
the spit of me at fourteen, kennelled in the attics.

It's more than the pleasure of a well-kept façade,
seen for years from a moving car on a stale main street –
this archway to a paved close, with lighted trees in pots,
like something glimpsed in an old town in Spain,
where houses turn inwards to stone courtyards
left by the Romans or the Caliphate.

A DECONSECRATED FURNITURE SHOWROOM

The high glass hall's left empty, but a notice
guides the pilgrim to the upstairs café.
*The restaurant will continue to trade
in spite of the recklessness of their banking partners
and their agents.*

Shaded lanterns hang on long chains
like relics in the cathedral of Toledo,
the private dining room is screened
and locked as any royal side chapel,
and the nave's a funnel of celestial light
within the shadowy void,
as the escalator carries you upwards,
a ladder of souls,
to frescoes, marble altars
sealed off with swags of tape.

The waitress tells me how the place shut down
and we say the words to each other,
receivership, jobs, recession
– antiphon, call and response –
but the faithful still meet in her upper room
over broccoli bake and apple tart, on breaks
from car dealerships and warehouses,
hospital wards across the roundabout.

IT'S

It's the way the garden clouds over of a sudden,
an abrupt wind slaps at your legs,
rattles the petals off the roses.

It's drawers lying open in the kitchen,
exposing a rabble of lost things,
hard angles ready for bruises.

It's a smell of gas with no source
in present time – your hob's electric,
the swelling gasometers long dismantled.

It's the hush after switching off the landing light,
when the staircase takes a breath and holds it,
and your eyes open wide on the dark.

THE NIGHTMARE JOB

I've sent a note to the office, asking
to bury my child, and the answer is no,
I must not leave my class, the lesson must go on,
though it's too late for my baby, padded out
in his nappy and corduroys and jacket
with a woollen hat to keep him warm
– but he is cooling now, and soon he'll stiffen.

I can't lay my son down without a blanket
to soften the floor's carpet tiles and concrete.
I want him with me, so I prop him sitting up
on the wide windowsill, leaning on the glass
between the classroom and the street.

The sky's grey light's enough to dim the truth,
which will burst and annihilate me
if they ever let me carry him out of here.

Coming To

And then you notice the clock hand tapping,
wheelie bins rolled between gable and lorry,
your own first movement, neck and knuckles creaking,
a rumble of wind in the branches, a spoonful of cereal
pinking the bowl, two rooms away the kettle growling
in the kitchen where he is up and doing,
the hanky fanfare from his stuffed-up nose

– sleep clears, and something presses on your hearing
as if the world is breathing in your ears,
or a two-bar electric fire is gulping heat
out of a socket in a long-ago rattle house,
a shaded bulb in the middle of the ceiling,
willow-pattern wallpaper figures repeating.

STRANGE BEDS

The guest room where you wake
rearranges itself in your mind – the gap
where the door is set, the walls, the curtains,
all shuffling into position, realigning,
adapting to the dream of current reality.

What might a real exile do to you
when even a small one knocks you off
the default settings where you're snug,
switches the temperature to less or more
than your body can nod to, and still get on
with self-location? Like the inscriptions
you used to find on flyleaves with the full
name and address of the teenage reader
starting with the number of the house
and ending in The World, The Universe.

The head, your head, on an unfamiliar pillow,
too hard or too soft, struggles to place itself,
and the limbs, your limbs, move among the sheets
like ivy suckers trying to attach
to jaggy pebbledash. Where are you now?
If you close your eyes you could be anywhere.

Heavy Rain, Low Light

This murky morning needs the lamp turned on,
but what's to stop me sitting up in bed
watching wet leaves sparkle beyond glass,
with three pillows at my back, my feet stuck out
to the hot water bottle's remaining heat
in my padded envelope of quilt and mattress?

I've been saving myself for a dark and rainy day,
my bright hoard concealed by branches,
a hedge against the theft of time,
saved-up daylight, my trunk of minutes
to be spent, whatever I do, by nightfall.

The rain collects its light in millions,
floods river valleys, fills the newspapers,
draws a shining beaded veil
across the window of my lamp-lit lair.

Nobody expected, nothing to be done,
food in the fridge and oil in the tank.
The power lines are still ok.
I hear the boiler singing below stairs.

WHAT DID YOU SAY?
Asda, Downpatrick

While the till extrudes my coiled receipt
I'm making small talk for the checkout man
penned in his hatch by the conveyor belt.

Getting busy now? is all I'm asking,
but he responds *the building is sinking
into the marshes* as if the two of us

are conspirators with codes and passwords
exchanging news of dangers met or planned.
He smiles, he nods, he shrugs, he sweeps

a hand towards the dipping car park
in a gesture from an opera's revelation,
to the orange barriers and repair signs

shoring up the ground of all our commerce
against stirrings of the earth in peaty reed beds.
Under the paving, the beach. Under the tarmac, the bog.

KNEE ARTHROSCOPY

What do you understand of this? A Beckett line
from one of the team in blue scrubs, her mouth
moving in a face revealed like a nun's
inside the frame of her boiled cotton wimple.
My clumsy answer seems to be enough
to signify informed consent.

Weeks later, two small scratches show their working out
– nib marks, dashes, brackets enclosing
a missing parenthesis, an hour's oblivion,
the skin invisibly mended, as the physio
explains how long it takes for hidden scars
to bind and stretch –

pointing at a wall poster of a human figure
imagined as a cut-out doll, skinned and neat
with layered outfits of fat and muscle, bone
and gristle, ligaments crisscrossing the kneecap
like the elastic girdles worn by women in my youth
to restrain unruly flesh.

Here's me, a worn pop-up book of the body.
She says they *cut down through tissue*
to clear loose fragments where I'd gone to pieces,
to pare away roughnesses accrued
by years of use, to smooth the torn edges
of insult and injury.

SHRUB APTITUDES

What you and I meant, what he, she and they meant,
comes out skew-ways, like sentences
bricked up one word at a time by beginners
dodging plagiarism with dictionary Lego,
in essays co-authored with Dada and Webster,
where *equity is onerous and surmised*, and *bush craft*
turns into *shrub aptitudes (vital for survival).*

Straight from the womb to a world of words and faces,
pulled towards a tone of voice, a look, a chosen phrase,
still we don't quite translate into each other,
though we live until we die in the attempt,
putting it one way, then another, until aptitude
meets craft, and shrubs re-wild to aboriginal bush.

DARK TOURISM
Irish Workhouse Centre, Portumna

We can't have hanging baskets or a coffee shop.
There were no flowers here.
Our guide puts on her coat to go inside.

Here's the mother and baby room.
Just imagine, says she to us,
as we stand buttoned up in the cold,
and we know we cannot, but we do.
Look at these windows. Now young man,
why do you think they are set so high?

A shadow listens for movement on the stones,
for footsteps learned by heart, a voice
among many heard through a window
set above the mothers' heads.

When the baby's second year is at an end,
and she is able to totter by herself,
she'll be taken away to walk on the rough yard
with the last of her sisters,
parted at the poorhouse door.

The girls sing kitchen songs and lullabies,
laments they may live to carry
from a tumbled home into service or America,
with the old prayers, though even in the chapel
the men, the women, the sons, the daughters,
are never in sight of each other.

There was no wonder made of death here.
Shadows follow our guide from room to room.
Her son rings at the wrong time from Australia.
Her winter coat is not enough.
Her breasts ache. Her hot heart pains her.

THE OTHER MYRRHA

Her newborn boy was fine, considering, but afterwards
she wouldn't look at him or hold him. You've heard
of that thousand-yard stare? The baby was so cute
we midwives nicknamed him Adonis.

Her confidential file has all the backstory. The kid's name
was Myrrha; her dad, Cinyras, a donor
to every good cause and the ruling party;
her mother, Cenchreis, a youthful beauty.
As their darling fairy grew into a pouting teen,
with a lovely little figure for her age, her mum got jittery,
criticised Myrrha's clothes and mentioned *jailbait*

– but her dad would offer drinks and tell her friends
what men preferred, poke fun at spotty boys,
say teenage girls were *so much more mature.*
Myrrha had a secret to torment her, twisting the bedsheets
as she lay alone, pondering her father's view
that these things should be learned at home
– look how, in many cultures, girls were taught
such private arts by older men who knew
what they were doing, not their clumsy peers –
surely his princess was worthy of no man
more than her daddy who knew what was best.
In the animal kingdom, billy goats and bulls
would have their way with any available female,
including their own offspring, and sire young.
It felt good, didn't it? So how could it be wrong?

She practised her own pleasure, conjuring
Cinyras' words, his hands, his eyes on her,
until it came to cutting lines on her limbs,
a little minor bloodletting, therapeutic
as far as it went, and that is how the housekeeper
caught her out while her bewildered mother

was away on a pilgrimage with the ladies of the parish.
This temp her father hired was used to sourcing girls,
and knew he liked them fresh – men will be men
– so soothed and sweet-talked Myrrha,
led the youngster to her parents' dim-lit bedroom,
where one side of the kingsize bed was vacant,
and Cinyras had chilled champagne.
He refilled the teenager's glass till she was giddy,
murmured *baby*, pretended not to know
whose voice replied. And to tell the truth, he did
know what to do – unhappy joy! After a week of this,
her tongue tasted of metal, the first sign
that she would be a mother to her brother.

On the ninth night Cinyras heard his wife come home
from her devotions and let herself in. The lights came on.
He shouted, *Myrrha! What are you doing? Get out of my bed,*
you slut! and lashed out fast to silence her, but Myrrha
dodged his fists, sprinted away, hitched to the city,
ate at soup kitchens, walked lighted streets by night, slept
in doorways by day, evaded do-gooders,
concealed the bump – afraid to live, afraid to die.

At home they whispered, *what a little madam!*
Cinyras and Cenchreis reared a cuckoo. Of course
he didn't know! He was asleep, tired out, poor breadwinner.
They spoilt her rotten. Next she'll appear in some enquiry,
accusing her own father, the drugged-up hussy!
Cenchreis doubled her visits to the House of Prayer.
The clergy were especially sympathetic.
And that's how Myrrha came to us at St Lucina's,
numb and speechless, wooden-faced from shock.
The baby went into care, the girl to a hostel,
leaking milk at first, then silent tears

– institutionalised, an icon, a moving statue
– wiping the communal kitchen, mopping the floors.

SHAME

There's a bad smell on the stairs,
in the angle of a landing where steps
reverse, you're going nowhere,
can't see your way clear.

You can trace its moment
rising slowly on each tread,
turning your head and sniffing
for danger on the wind.

Try the shelf of specimens,
pebbles, antlers, shells and mermaids' purses.
Put your head into the basket of ironing.
Look underfoot for forgotten stains.

You may locate the very spot
head height in unmarked paintwork at a corner,
something foul within the structure
that will always be beyond you.

THE POOL OF BLOOD
after William Degouves de Nuncques

Perhaps you know this stand of trees,
shedding darkness by a lit shrine
where old paths cross.
Yew trees leaning inward,
a canopy or baldachino
over a pond, a pool of blood.

Its colour does not deepen:
this blood is always fresh,
on the battlefields, the roadsides,
the hospitals, the soaked beds,
under the cobbles of marketplaces,
the flagstones of town squares.

When the explosion meets the crowded street,
and you regret your colour television,
this is where the blood goes,
seeping down below the paving
to the core of the earth.

After the firemen finished, and her blackened room
cooled, she returned in daylight
to find what was left. Vinyl records melted,
but the cloth toy lion was only maimed,
smelling of petrol and slightly charred.

Dogs growled in the street and the talk
inside the houses was no smoke without fire,
but she went back alone to sleep with her fear,
having decided to be innocent,
stretched out in a clean bed saved from the pyre –
until the folded, hand-delivered note
from someone who spelt Fenian *bitchs*
slowly, tongue out, missing an e,
scoring deeply into thin-lined paper.
Next time we burn your house you will be in it.

At night in the new place,
only drunken singers, swaying home,
banged at her heart and woke her. Still and all,
it took three years of clearing space
before the nightmares could move in,
under the quilt she brought back from her travels,
where the lion used to sit, front legs upright,
paws flexed and ready, his wool mane still unsinged.

THE PEACE-AND-QUIET BOARD
for Andy

The day of the move, the six-year-old said
now are we going back to sleep
in our own house tonight?

When all this is over, she meant –
packing crockery in newspaper,
manoeuvring sofas round door jambs

and unscrewing the plywood window blind
– a shield against stone throwing, or worse –
that you cut and drilled and bolted to the sill,
a sturdy panel between Moses basket and glass,
concealed from the street by rosebud curtains,
concealed from the children by talk of soundproofing
and a name, *the peace-and-quiet board.*

That first night here, do you remember, you and I
slept on a mattress in the living room –
crackling nylon carpet, giddy with orange swirls –
and lay in the corner, holding on tight to each other?

In the end you sawed and sandpapered that barricade
for a table-football game of tuppenny players,
flicked with fingertips into a utopia
of treaties signed with fountain pens
on brassbound polished tables.

FLAG PROTESTOR

When he first gave up on holding high the banner,
he pinched the corners together,
drawing it to his collar like a warrior
in some poor illustration of the Ulster cycle.

He should have hair squared off at the shoulder,
a blunt fringe above pale eyes
that he shields from the light with knuckly fingers
as he scans the horizon from his hillside shelter.

He should wear a tunic of brownish wool,
rough woven like sacking,
dyed with onion skins,
held at the waist with a belt of deer sinews,
plaited before they cooked its flesh
among hot stones in the hunting season.
He should have oatmeal and honey and stories.

SECURITY
for Jeff Collins

Where was it I read that after Chinese emperors
were long gone, knees still buckled at the sight
of a Party official, and it was all the poor
people could do to stop themselves kowtowing?

Remember dropping to the ground at a bang
from a car exhaust in some English high street,
showing opened bags in chain-store doorways,
checking all kerbs for unattended cars?

As infants' mouths turn to a fingertip,
we were hand reared for spycam and scanner,
suspected, monitored, bad with our nerves,
arms held out in prayer or surrender.

Leaving for England the first time, my cabin trunk
arrived in college by boat a fortnight after I did.
Two weeks of grateful breathing, alone in my locked room,
two weeks of startling men, just by saying hello,
not knowing that I was a young woman, therefore
small town courtesies would be taken for seduction.
And once the trunk was unfastened,
I saw what I had packed: black skirts
such as a nun might wear when habits were relaxed,
wrapped round six jars of my mother's gooseberry jam,
like the food left in coffins to keep the dead going,
crossing over into the great beyond.

Leaving for England years later to visit the grandparents
of our hybrid children with their transplanted father,
the car boot is searched at the docks for explosives and
found instead to contain several loaves of wheaten bread
– and here is what the searcher said.
They all pack bread. You can't get decent bread in England.

ACCENTUATED

It takes a while to learn the shift to normal,
but when you first go there, no time at all
to note that they think you put on difference
for entertainment, like the grass-skirted dancers
the Commonwealth exhibits to its visiting queen.

Because you love to hear new voices,
language you've only come across in books,
the first time a posh girl cries *rah-thaah!*
you jump up, thrilled as Darwin on the Beagle,
until scorn and outrage freeze her face.

So you take to observation in concealment,
although almost every one of them you meet
is distracted by the quaintness of your accent,
which they cannot help believing you maintain
to make the point that you refuse to be normal.

LONDON IRISH
for Gretta Mulrooney

They called their neighbours *the cockneys*,
and every summer gathered saved-up money
for the Holyhead boat, and then the drive
across the Bog of Allen, where every village
had its own song that the mother sang –
    the main street is a row of trees
    where the liars dwell as thick as thieves –
to sons and daughters wedged in the back seat,
looking sideways at green letterboxes with ER
painted over, at the cream and emerald trim of post offices
whose signs said *Oifig an Phoist* in Gaelic-revival script,
small shops with bacon slicers on the counter
where they'd pop the crown cork off your mineral
and wheedle for details of seed, breed and generation,
to place you on the map of townlands and reputation,
family feuds, *where is it he is now,*
indexing the archives of the lost and the returned.

TANNOY IN THE TERMINAL

This is a place of waiting between worlds.
Your passport will remind you who you're meant to be.

Your carry-on holdall is for holding all
you cannot do without in this land or the next.

While you scan departure screens for omens,
take care not to leave your past unattended.

Once you have been through the queue for security,
please make the effort to feel more secure.

At any moment you may be required
to set off towards a gate to another life.

Until then, we implore you, relax and shop.

THE MAN ON THE PLANE

He has a look of Mr Potato Head – blue-eyed, brush-cut,
over-filling the seat between me and his mother,
who nods to me, eighty-two he says, sharp as a knife,
even after her fall, but not fit for the escape door,
so while they wait to be moved, he tells me all about
the Spanish holiday he paid for, with not a single thank-
you from the fucken sister who is fucken selfish
and never comes near the mother,
who kept her in money all through the divorce.
The mother would give you anything.
She'd fucken give you her arse and shite through her ribs.

PLEASE STUDY THE SAFETY CARD

A recorded announcer warns *brace, brace!*
and our seat card shows a faceless woman
looking into an infant's empty face.
She is preparing to die in her stockinged feet,
folded forward with one hand on her head,
the other hugging her baby to her right breast
– holding the child tight in the crook of her arm.

If our air supply should fail, oxygen masks
will drop like manna or propaganda leaflets
on a mother with white socks and a pony tail,
touching her neatly-outlined boy
perhaps for the last time, pulling on her mask,
then his, her palm on his crown
for the feel of his final haircut.

The flight attendant is drawn as stocky,
his waistcoat strained around the tummy
as he leans to pull the cord on the escape chute,
and by my exit, one of the cartoon men
– short back and sides with a hint of quiff –
is wrenching off the hatch cover,
throwing away my emergency door,
stepping out into a wash of blue.

NOTICE FOR THE INCHKEITH LIGHTHOUSE OPTIC
National Museum of Scotland

This seat is placed for marvelling.
Tilt your head back to see
the huge dioptic lens by David Alan Stevenson, engineer,
whose cousin Robert Louis
took his stories to distant lands
while the rest built lighthouses for humanity
in Scotland and Japan.
Made in eighteen-eighty-nine
by Chance Brothers of Birmingham,
and in the holy spirit
of James Dove and Company, Edinburgh,
stately clockwork spinning
on polished cogs of steel and brass
under a louvred cupola of crystal,
to guide sea travellers to the port of Leith
– safe passage and the mark of home.

When the lamp begins to burn,
the lantern may appear
about to levitate, as if a gentle wind
set off its tiny flame. Look how the light
turns and is mirrored, refracted
– daily adjustment and repair maintaining
its reach and spread, its firework flash,
the machinery of tenderness.

KEEP CLEAR

Attend to the sea as it shushes your objections,
casting yellow plastic bottles back on shore,
massaging the gravel and striated bedrock
collapsed along its fault lines aeons before.

Breathe as if pedalling slowly in sunlight,
playing the handlebars, towing a dog alongside,
or resting a boat in its home-made marina,
consenting to daily shifts of pebbles and tide.

Follow shoals of fish the size of little fingers,
dodging like a tickle among boulders and weed,
pouring themselves clear from dazzle into shadow.
Attend, breathe, follow – can this be all you need?

ON A BATHROOM WALL IN ROME

This window is kept open: the catch sticks.
Take care not to drop items into the courtyard
four storeys below, especially if awakened
at three am when nightingales
renew their legendary song
during the break in traffic before dawn

– if you must lean out, entranced,
holding your mobile phone set to record,
saving this wonder to your sim card,
observe all reasonable precautions,
but do not neglect to murmur, *Philomel.*

WE WISH TO EVOKE A SENSE OF THE AUTHENTIC
Masson Mills, Derbyshire

Deep Water   One Way Only
    a hundred lights keep busy on the weir
    as in the darker nights of eighteen-forty
ladybirds overwintering on the Danger sign
    since Arkwright brought his horse in out of the rain
    and cotton bales came cheap from the Americas

Push Open the Double Doors
    to a stalactite cave of bobbins and spindles
hung with six thousand eight hundred and forty samples
and find your foothold among spilling sacks
        think of Dziga Vertov   Rumplestiltskin
    or the clutter of ex-votos at a shrine

Exit To The Riverbank
    where boilers set their faces like masks of truth
    fanned frown lines on their foreheads
    the round eyes of tinderbox dogs
    Moloch mouths greedy for children

Some Objects Are Dangerous   Take Care
    to complicate your tour we have displayed
    found objects on a theme of manufacture
    metal troughs with battered lips
    rusty forceps   cleaver and spade
a single tiny boot may make you pause
    but this child's clog was not found here

No Access to the Past Beyond This Point

BED POST PLEASE TOUCH
Victoria and Albert Museum

Next to the table made of resin,
3D printed, with fractals
coded to resemble a tree,

a remnant of a Regency four-poster
listed as a touch object,
not as Jamaica wood

from saw logs dragged to ships
by people with no names
but monogrammed skin

– what traces survive
in a bed for coupling,
conceiving, birthing, leaving,

if hands pick up the charge of lives
rubbed to a polish,
births, deaths, marriages?

She cries out, grabs the bed post's
swags and curlicues
in turned mahogany,

sends out a fine-grained shiver
to shock my own flesh
– human conduction.

SET OF LITURGICAL TOYS 1880–1890
Victoria and Albert Museum

On birthdays and on prosperous Christmases
sons bred for priesthood might unwrap
these silver miniatures
– ciborium, monstrance, thurible –
a dolls' tea set for pious boys
playing Melchisidech before the mirror,

opening this gilt-edged missal bound in black leather
with a stitched ribbon to mark the place
in the liturgical year,

unfolding tiny vestments in the colours decreed
for Easter, Advent, Epiphany,
red for Sundays of the Holy Innocents,
white for the burials of unbaptised children,
violet for blessings, and for penitence.

IN THE ARMOURY OF THE KNIGHTS OF MALTA
Valletta

We pay to see exoskeletons emptied of flesh,
absences forged from shadows

– helmets to make a face into a death's head,
pelmeted brows, their stare of solid force,

chain mail *ganseys* worn with pikes,
breastplates embellished with the lives of saints,

bucklers, greaves, blunt-toed iron shoes
in bear paw form, etched with acanthus leaves,

and here, a metal suit, round-bellied skirted weskit
and reticulated open-crotch leggings,

bespoke to fit the warm, well-muscled thigh,
tapering to a neat knee, of one long dead.

Who was he, unfastened, in his bed,
this swaggerer whose shape is left behind?

A Business Meeting at the Slieve Donard Hotel

A British Irishman and a French Londoner
meet by the seaside at a newfangled railway hotel
in the reign of King Edward and his cousin Leopold;
velvet curtains muffling Ulster voices of children
on the sand and bathers in the chilly waves.
As words fly out across the gold-rimmed cups, each breath
vanishes into the polished air of the Grand Coffee Room.

Their letters start *Dear Tiger* and *Dear Bulldog*.
Clandestine still, let's give them other names. Mr Frame
from the Foreign Office longs to be undiplomatic,
throwing full daylight on the filthy crimes of power,
and Mr Shroome has left his bills of lading
suppurating in a back office on the quays of Antwerp,
shipping ledgers rotting down to feed connections,
spreading underground like a mycelium net
for growing outrage – photography and book-keeping –
imports of ivory and rubber in one column,
exports of whips, chains and ammunition in the other.

Mr Shroome's descendants march with banners, chanting
Protect the Human. The tides return and chandeliers
still shine for guests at conferences, weddings
and civil partnerships. Mr Frame's diaries
are no longer enough to justify a hanging.

Perhaps a castle is burnt out by an angry crowd
as the drums bangbang *The People!*
United! Will Never Be Defeated!

unless the castle is taken instead for the assembly
to rule by acclaim before interlocking betrayals
choke its pipework and rot its floors,

until it falls out of use and into disrepair
and is refurbished by a later government
as an official summer residence

complete with parkland, swans, geese, gleaming mallards,
an artificial waterfall and lake,
a smooth parterre with trimmed hedges,

and then the castle can be passed to the survivors
for a museum of revolution to visit on fine evenings,
with lightshows and a guillotine in the garden.

A VIEW

I never believed in foreign scenes on postcards
after John Hinde's glossy Ireland with its turquoise sky,
framed by an arch of branches, a golden mean
of pink rhododendron that the photographer
must have carried around in the boot of the car.

I'm sticking stamps on photos to send home
but they smell of cardboard and you can't see
streetlights below the trees at evening
hung with bunches of yellow bead berries
– or notice a girl in flat shoes walk past,
downcast eyes and heavy swaying hair,
her scarlet lipstick and scarlet duffel coat
telling you she looked in the mirror before leaving

– or enter the market hall, named for the day bombs fell,
tiled with shining fruit and a plaque to count the dead,
or hear the music, Arabic or Spanish, in a minor key
from an upstairs window above the pavement
where cars growl past and people talk loudly
in words you don't understand, in tones you do

– you can't smell dinners cooking in the kitchens,
or resin and herbs on the hill ringing the castle
where you take the lift to the summit to drink coffee
from the courtyard kiosk and read
a notice fixed there in three languages
with the municipal crest

– *until opened to the public in the 1960s*
the castle was used as a prison, a concentration camp
and a shelter for the homeless –

centuries beyond the picturesque.

For A Guide to Sardinia

Future towns of coal and silver
– Carbonia, Argenteria –
the one he called Mussolinia after himself,
and Fertilia, where anything might grow.
If hotel space is scant it makes
a reasonable place to sleep.

The dictator's notions of order
gave the town hall a watchtower,
drained swamps of mosquitoes,
but also egrets,
took people like cuttings to plant
in sticky malarial silt,
a model village of grids and blocks,
a sketch on squared paper.

Children and dogs play in its streets.
The past is filtered out of them,
as reeds around the town's lagoon
suck filth and breathe it out again,
sweetened for the fishing lines
men fasten to the ruined Roman bridge,
a foreground for your photographs.

THE DANISH RESISTANCE MUSEUM

From the kingdom of bicycles and Lego,
here's a little scaled-down armoured car,

scrap-metal nixer from the railway yard,
cardboard-grey, Frit Danmark in red on the bonnet,
the gun hatch unevenly cut out
like a cereal packet model made in nursery class.

You want to smile and pat its sides
as you might a sleeping dog,
or a plaything left behind when childhood's gone
– this vehicle a tight fit, right enough,
for a grown Dane with a loaded gun
sticking out like a Dalek's armpiece
in wartime woods where fellow citizens
claimed Aryan supremacy in blood.

A Sunny Day at Chef de Baie

Someone photographed an execution here
– a firing squad, a priest, no blindfold.

Under blue awnings, the beach café tables
are full. The special is mussels and chips.

A memorial stone lists all the names.
Their flag flies every day, but they are dead.

Some were communists, some Christians.
Most were tortured. Others heard the screams.

Ten yards away, our cars are closely parked,
steering wheels searing in holiday heat.

They were young, enjoying the summer.
That's what the words on the noticeboard said.

Girls in cute bikinis run on the sand.
Families unpack towels and picnic baskets.

Against barbarity, we fortify
our settlements, our tide-washed sandcastles.

SNCF SAYS FRÊT

Distant trains swipe hourly past the hedge,
skimming over our house-exchange garden
with a boom to burst the Burgundian quiet,
their streaming bulk ripping a watercolour sky
that repairs itself behind each zippered slash,
until the next train tears into the horizon.

Which rolling stock this time? Passenger coaches
painted blue for summer trips, cartoon clouds
and happy children's faces? Sealed-box containers
loaded at the docks? Tankers of chemicals?

But when they send these chains of wagons
with livery marked *FRÊT* in large slanting letters,
urgent, imperative, though it's just *freight* in French
– already I've seen, obeyed and started to fret.

These carriages are too familiar, crudely planked,
roofed over, trundling slowly on the track,
rough trucks to carry goods or cattle. People
were herded on this railway, standing all the way,
unfed, terrified, shitting where they stood,
the whole map webbed with final journeys,
one-way excursions to the East.

A City-Break in Lyon
Your duty is to disobey – Charles Péguy

Later we'll visit the puppets – we will need them,
among the city's histories, its lists of things to see
and do, museums and collections, restaurants
with plaster piglets in the windows,
and we must hurry as we haven't long.

First we peep in at miniatures, through glass,
faces carved from conkers, a ship from a tooth,
a dolls' house likeness of a vacated bedsit
– an after-image of a dawn denied –
the artist working by slow exhalations
so that his hand does not tremble,
troubling to honour the patches of damp on the ceiling,
keeping his first white hairs as guitar strings
for an orchestra of ants.

The textile museum sets golden fish swimming
on blue silk from third century Egypt,
but the forests of the Beaux Arts are full of babies
seized from naked, screaming women.

Before the puppets comes a duty.
Calm and silence are required.
This zone is not recommended
for children or the sensitive.
In the old Gestapo barracks, we see, but must not
speak. We contemplate evidence, handwritten letters
denouncing undesirables, we venerate
relics, the Hollywood mouth of Jean Moulin
and we peer through a pane of glass in the floor
that is also the ceiling of Barbie's cellar,
stopping to view clips of witnesses
at the trial where he had nothing to say.

Now we may find our way to the puppets,
rooms full of antique automata
fixed to dioramas like a population bewitched,
peeling turnips by clockwork, carrying water,
treading grapes as if for export in Barbie's war,
while the city's Mr Punch, Citizen Guignol,
did not betray his neighbours,
but saw what he must see.

An Irishwoman Reads *Dodo* with Keith Douglas

Any dusty tent can be made beautiful
with flowers and books in a cut-out petrol can,
such as the tank men fill with desert sand
as bricks to make small houses for latrines.

In spite of his photographed moustache
and his few years of manliness, he is excited
by tinned rations jazzed-up for squadron dinners.
An acceptable hot porridge can be made
of hammered biscuits, boiled and laced with jam.

He's careful of the whiskey. He must stay fit
to note the fear that pushes at his belly, just
where the shell would enter, and his useless pity
for the burnt corpse of one who'd laid a towel
over his wounds against tormenting flies.

In hospital after the landmine, the young captain
needs the book they bring – he reads it twice –
Dodo, Edwardian comfort to draw his poet's eye
away from the wreckage of flesh and the ends of bone.

I find it on my Kindle and I read *Dodo* too
at bedtime in his honour, by its faded glow,
saving his *Zem Zem* for sensible daylight
– the boy learned how to kill and soon was dead
as a doornail, blown to glory, joined the majority.

THE USES OF SILK

These days the best of combat underwear
is made from silk in Fivemiletown, County Tyrone.

But among the petticoats of hill-farm women,
silkworm pupae rode through centuries
of ice and snow in the southern Alps
on the stride of a warm thigh,
until picked off into boiling water,
corpses unwound from cocoons of silken thread
for bolts of rich cloth sold in the valleys.

And a Chinese waistcoat of yellow spider silk
was five years' labour for eighty people
in glasshouses littered
with the sucked-out husks of bluebottles,
each spinner high-five to a man's palm,
generations of golden orb spiders
spooling draglines of finery,
stronger than the fiercest filament
dreamt of in modern war's laboratories.

Now, look, in khaki dust the captain's shouting
Your front man is a blind man
– keep to the safe lane –
someone's watching through a murder hole
– so I want every fucker
thinking what they're doing!

Young men with our English in their mouths
dressed up by armour scientists
in military underwear, privates cocooned
in a shrapnel-catching net of silk,
the soft answer that turns away wrath.

WHEN NIGHT COMES DOWN

Windows blacken, and the train takes on
a dreamy badness, something not right
  – a fluorescent strip switched on by dusk
can't lighten this dark where we are not at home
  under the dim roof, our faces odd, unwell, afraid,

like refugees, held apart from our lives,
  crossing borders, keeping ready, getting our story straight,
pausing in a no-place where we hope to be carried
  to safety, clutching our tickets, checking what's left
with an eye to the doors, unable to let our minds
  wander for long into the orchards of the past,
brought back to this bad light, to greyed-out stares
  reflected in black windows blind with grit,
moving down the timetable on an iron road,
  its rails set by crews with torches, trudging the tracks
on nights of broken journeys, skirting round the shit
  flushed from ageing trains, the smell of travellers' distress
washed down by rain marbled with leaked diesel,
  off gravel and steel and into the water table.

THE FEAST OF THE EPIPHANY AND THE BALLAST OFFICE CLOCK

Now for the women's Christmas, the twelfth day,
when glitter and mistletoe are put away
as we face into the headwind of the year,
outrunning time, denying all delay,
packing Jesus in his manger's hay
with eggbox bells preserved from Primary One,
their flaking paint and paper-mash decay.

Where is the magic star we must obey?
The soulful, sudden clock to shine our way,
ticking out today, today, today?
While Caspar, Balthasar and Melchior
fail to send Herod's murder squads astray,
too late again to sing *lullay, lullay,*
we'll shred the tree, unplug the coloured lights,
bubblewrap our baubles while we may.

INTERRAIL
for Joy Kelly Moore

The tired boy sharing her seat looked into her eyes
the day they took him off the Budapest train.

Now wood pigeons *coocoo* in the hotel garden
as a lizard traverses a wall and makes no noise,
and in the time it takes for nail polish to dry
some day is saved, some life is lost,

while she reads a magazine whose cover promises
to ask celebrities how one can be happy,
a piece on seagulls with a taste for landfill,
and an exquisite photo of psychedelic sewage,
marbling a canal in swirls of purple and green.

Megaliths echo for her two hands clapping,
as hummingbird hawkmoths flicker in the hedge.
Unobserved, she rinses her fingers in the font
of a church in a foreign street, by a mural
of Germaine Tillion, home from Ravensbrück,
who kept a good table for guests and lived to a hundred.

Barbed wire enclosures are under construction
beside railway lines on several borders.

She will think of that boy as long as she lives.
How will her own house be remembered?

A CURSE ON A CABINET MINISTER
after James Stephens and Dáithi Ó Bruadair

May you be left with not enough coins for a phone call
and have to live in a hostel, on your uppers
in a country where you don't know the language,
in a room that smells of damp and has six people in it
with all their possessions stacked on bunks, and a kitchen
with no lock on the fridge, and may your only books
be an anthology of laments for the dispossessed,
and a copy of *Hard Times* by Charles Dickens
with the Gradgrind bits marked out in dayglo green.
May your own music be forbidden to you,
and when you crave a smile, a handshake, an *after you*
gesture as you stumble onto the bus, may it take you
to a detention centre full of banished scholars
who tell you all they've learned. May you wake up there
under a communal ceiling whose perpetual light
illuminates the corners of your ignorance.

THE COLD CHAIN

With numbers ticking backwards on the clock
until the months of watching find their price,
most of Europe's cut flowers are sold at Schipol
in an auction that it takes a year to learn
– bellflowers for a street stall, roses for Valentines,
night-scented stock like embroidered tea-cosies
– bid for against time, like copper futures
on the trading floor, then flown to stopovers
on snowy tarmac at Murmansk,
or Spanish loading bays in oven heat
that bounces off the ground, a kerosene shimmer
trapped among petals that sag and wither,
losing their bloom of money and desire.

Just wasted carbon, so why did it move me
to hear how the factory team put on the kettle
at the manager's house, pushed back toys and sofas
to make space, and packed the boss
time and again into a cargo trolley, pulled
their thermal sleeve around him, a capsule
muffled against polar chill and killing sun,
and closed him up to test for chinks of light?

Could it have been the feeding bottle,
flecked with the lunch hour's expressed milk,
that I swaddled in wet cotton to stay cool for my return,
the sceptical childminder, my baby's searching mouth?

Or was it the isolation cell where hunger
kicked her to the floor, and young Irina
wore a quilted waistcoat, made by prisoners
adding scraps of cloth torn off over years
in the small zone, enough to warm
her heart and lungs, and keep alive
God and poems moving in her blood?

BORDERING

The native Irish birch is enough to fill a window,
winter branches pluming, holding up
our washing line and nest box,
ringing the years before and after ceasefires.

This side of the glass, a Chinese pound shop cat
is patting the air each second with its golden paw,
ready to knock fists for luck when we come in,
long-lashed human eyes painted wide open

– staring at rolling news
as flags change twice in two days,
observing shot and shell and stumbling people
– the clenched paw waves to a reporter
pointing at Scutari on a map,
salutes the antiques expert who is holding
Miss Nightingale's lamp, her workman's lantern,
a flame-lit cylinder of pleated linen
bought in the bazaar at Constantinople,
just like those still sold in Istanbul.

THREE BEDROOMS

Because it was their only private place
Santa's haul was hidden under my parents' bed
near the lamp with black-and-white whiskey dogs,
and the immovable wardrobe in solid oak
they made together in their early days
at a night class taught by my father's friend,
who chose a design my mother would hate forever.

Because it was the cheapest kind, we bought
a folding table for pasting wallpaper
to use as a desk at our room's bay window.
An alarm clock on the marble mantelpiece
over the blocked-off fireplace, a jug of daffodils,
a piano we could not play, a red wool blanket
on that early bed, too small for both of us together.

Because the early light stays in the garden,
a white rocking chair holds out its arms
to curtains laced with gulls and lighthouses,
a cherry tree gone feral, twined with honeysuckle,
neighbours' windows, the dark gradient of forest,
and our raft of a bed with us in it together,
in reach of books, specs, earphones and each other.

WITH THIS RING

His wedding ring's gone from the button jar,
so long ago it's been forgotten.
Perhaps it was thrown out with the rubbish,
or will turn up when both of us are dead,
and one of our babies, getting on by then,
takes a turn at sorting out possessions.

That broad, scratched metal band may rattle
out of a posthumous shoebox, stuffed with letters.
Someone may wear it, or find it a nuisance
as he did, snagging when rock climbing
or washing up, and put it away again
among obsolete coins and unmatched keys.

Because he said that they reminded him
of nose rings for leading cattle,
we held off buying rings, so that an hour
before the wedding, we were running hand-in-hand
down an English high street to the cheapest shop
in red gingham and a borrowed shirt,
leaving two long-wedded couples
about to become parents-in-law unto death
to meet without an introduction
on the register office lawn.

FORMERLY

They will be grandparents, and the country
where they honeymooned will no longer exist,
after several wars, massacres, forced migrations,
the splitting and sorting of territories,
new dialects: a language whisked together
in official dictionaries will have separated out
like a curdled sauce, and worshippers
will devote themselves to difference.

When everything's the future, all that year
they go each week to a class in Serbo-Croat,
planning their fortnight with a phrasebook,
which the newlyweds are carrying in summer
as they leave the hot glare of the street
to visit the famous mosque. An old caretaker
beckons them to follow, leads them
down stairways, unlocks heavy doors
one after another, takes them along passages
deep into the crypt, feeling their way
towards a hollow where he turns the iron key
in a wooden chest, lifts out a treasure to show
the colours and gilt of illuminated pages,
Arabic on the left, and Cyrillic on the right
– then opens his face and voice to sing
the sacred words to the strangers, a song
alive among the centuries, out of his time
and theirs, before the next catastrophe.

There will be grandparents who remember.

THE STORK

And here online is our tiny bubble-skulled alien,
making itself at home in a little hammock!
We wake in our borrowed bed to a sonar image,
a twelve-week scan of the womb where the new mother
and our own son have combined all of themselves
and those that went before them, gathered
together like savings in some cosmic kitty,
to conjure up this being, to invite it into the world,
happed-up against the hazards of the journey.
Here are held the scrolls, the codes, the memory
of our species and our clans. We're hearing bells
ringing out from spires and clock towers
as the dial is set to survival.

The museum of La Rochelle is showing a stork,
stuffed for display on its nest above the marshes
– the world is full of omens, our minds stuck on playback –
and the summer exhibition is called Monstrous.
Its posters ask: *you think this is normal?*
on a photo of a spiked puffer fish with curled lips.
Magnified insects, robots, mythical creatures
and a pair of full-term infants, immured
within glass cylinders, cords still attached,
their faces intent, like old men thinking long,
hunched into silence in thick jars, closed eyelids
swollen, lips in perfect Cupid's bows, skulls
squashed out of true, brains extruding
into preserving fluid so that the strands
look like beautifully-tied topknots.
A woman behind me says *Cabbage Patch Dolls.*
Offered in 1854 to the city's men of science, specimens
of the same anomaly that finished my first pregnancy.

I'm back – and ten weeks gone. It's night.
Alone in a sideward as the pains take hold,

I'm floating, buoyed up by all who wish me well,
then carried through the years from wreckage into shelter,
where storks feed in fertile wetlands, return
to nests on rooftops, airlift the newly-born
in slings held tightly in their bills.

AMULET

O look with kindness on this woman, who is cycling
at the moment as a double weight on the saddle,
this woman who's more than a vessel, though full
of every hope, gravid, round, enceinte, encircling,
who is carrying our grandson, whoever he may be,
bellied like a sail open to a strong wind, heading
towards a new life for all of us.

At the online warehouse of pious tat,
they're keen to sell this magic. *For an offering
of $17 or more we will send you a hand-packaged
half-ounce bottle of Blessed Mother Oil.*

She's wheeling forward, in full charge
of blessings. I shake off the old urge
to tie an amulet to her handlebars.

FINE RIGHTLY

Why don't we have a cross of folded reeds,
cartwheeling along our kitchen lintel? We want
to chant. We want a square of tin, stamped
with the image of a baby, to lay in a cave
in the mountains. We cannot help but know
of wounds no cures can heal, a woman
held in extremity, a trial by ordeal
which pins her to the edge of her power,
turns her inside out and back again.

In February, when it's all gone on too long
across the water, and we're pacing the house,
unable to do anything to help our son,
or his gallant girl, or their baby,
whose moving-in to life is so delayed
– we let ourselves be led by urges beyond reason
to fertility goddess tales, sham-Celtic rigmaroles
for a fruitful spring at Imbolc or the feast of Brigid.

Prayer's never a temptation, knowing fine rightly
there's no one there to hear – and yet
we trace the ancient spring to a rugby club
by a fingerpost to mark St Brigid's Well
where we set down our foolish rose.
The sacred water seeps from underground
behind locked gates with lorries and CCTV.

Away out to the graveyard, where the bones
of loving parents decay together, RIP,
and we're tidying up, pinching off dried leaves,
tucking new narcissi in the spaces.
The phone! It's done. A perfect child,
lifted to safety from his mother's womb.
She's well, she's smiling at her baby.

Our son now has a son. We're all reborn.
I lean against the car, crying and shaking,
overcome as any pilgrim.

SEASCAPE WITH PORTRAIT

As the sea swings you in its waves
like a child between parents, you're bracketed
in my camera screen, you're framed

by the boisterous tide that crashes
against the edges of the rocky cove,
by the apron of sand, the toasted bodies
of white people, suited and sunscreened
in their family groups, by the mysteries of geology
that formed this place, your maleness,
the ease of your body, your childhood
and mine on separate islands, the further mysteries
of reproduction that formed us, the blue
of reflected sky on choppy sea, the broad bay's
distance, the discreet horizon in its chiffon mist

and you're framed too within your secret self,
which sometimes thinks you could not do without me,
while knowing also at such moments
I am the one outside the frame.

INSTRUCTIONS FOR PICKING WILD STRAWBERRIES AT MURLOUGH

Working in pairs, search out a scooped-out hollow
this side of the shoreline, a dip among the dunes
where sky appears over the tops of sandhills,
holding the horizon high above your heads.

Step carefully uphill beyond the valley path,
on thin tracks laid by wild ponies
between spikes of marram grass and burnet roses.

Pause to look down until you find
spots of crimson under leaves. Pick the fruit
but do not eat before you have enough
to hold to each other's mouths, a favour
to light up tongues and open all your eyes.

SMALL PRINT ON A BOX OF CHOCOLATES

He gave her a pink miniature hatbox
inscribed with art nouveau gold letters,
containing six handmade chocolates
in fluted ruffs of gilded paper.
An Ulsterman who knows what women want.

That was the start of the whole thing,
courtship, wedding, babies, house,
his business taking him away so often,
silences between toast and marmalade,
hot operatic scenes, his declaration
of passionate love for a young man
he'd met in London in his other life,
the breaking of Wedgwood, biblical denunciation
from her father in his County Armagh pulpit,
rending of garments in the temples
of the law courts, the judgement.

LOVING AND GIVING

You meet a boy and give yourself to him.
He doesn't give himself to you. Perhaps he gives you one.
You give way to him, give in to his demands.
You give him your virginity. You lose it and he takes it.

At your wedding, your father gives you away,
joking, *I hope she doesn't give you any trouble.*
You marry and are given in marriage. They say
love means to give and not to count the cost.

Your parents give their blessing. The neighbours
give pairs of sheets. The word is he'd give anyone
the shirt off his back, but is also given to rages,
though women's gossip gives a false impression.

There has to be give-and-take. Does he give a damn?
Do you give your all? You should give ground, not give
as good as you get. You don't give up. You take
what you're given, even given what happens next.

Now you're given a chance to give birth, give life,
but his fists give the lie to romance, or give rise
to disputes. For every pair, a giver and a taker
– you're told to give him his due, give over complaining.

But he gives you hell and you give some thought
to escape. You might give him what for,
give him his marching orders, give him the boot,
give evidence, give the lot of them notice to quit.

You plan it, give voice to your fears, give your exit
your best shot. You don't give yourself airs or give
reason for suspicion. You give him the slip,
then save the child, take back the self you gave.

THE SLUG AND THE AMARYLLIS

The amaryllis is in flower for two weeks
with lavish mathematical beauty,
precision-timed to go off every spring,
exploding from rotted vegetable compost
in crimson velvet skirts,
a trumpet fanfare of petals,
a megaphone message from heaven.

Gardeners poison slugs that slither
around the amaryllis bed,
but the sex lives of slugs are a marvel
of divine symmetry,
aerial artistes of the erotic garden.

THE CAR AND THE MOON

I followed the moon home from a city
where streetlamps sparked across the river,
and behind the darkened cut-outs of the houses,
sky pulsed like a light box,
the car with me inside it swaying
under a full moon,
round and flat
as a pod of honesty,
always close ahead
against Madonna-blue that gathered depth,
flushing to cobalt, indigo,
ultramarine, paint box Prussian,
until only the mountains were black enough
to show darker than the sky.

Night had closed about me while I drove,
and when I pulled up the handbrake,
the moon's face shone with full intent
on the path to your door.

CARDIOLOGY

The years a present, the days lived in good heart.
That your days may be many, steady the beat of your
 heart.

Under your skin they stitched a shiny charm
to catch the perturbations of your heart.

An engine of flesh, a valved and chambered mill,
a pumping bloody fist, this heart.

Padded satin sold for Valentine's –
rose-petal curls, not the beetroot lump of a heart.

Written in sherbet, *I'm Yours!* rubs off on the tongue.
A game of fortunes, a sweetie, a Love Heart.

Clover and tormentil. Clanking cable cars.
Alps with failing glaciers at their heart.

Misled, you abseiled back three hundred feet.
Rope and luck held, past thirty years, dear heart.

No Diarmuid and Gráinne's Bed at the Plan du Praz,
but Rock Table Ridge is an epic you learned by heart.

All Our Pleasures Prove

Yes, maybe I will live with you a while
in a hut made of scraps lifted from skips
– ends of planking, splintery pallets,
corrugated iron and mossy perspex
torn from lean-to sheds
cleared for conservatories,
discarded worktops from outdated kitchens.

We'll fill our mattress with sheep's wool
collected from barbed wire fences,
brew tea in scoured tin cans
hung on coat hanger handles
over a beach fire of driftwood,
where the tide will wash the hot stones,

as we step among our salvage
on the edge of the shingle
in our garden of sea-cabbage and sea-pinks,
and you will save me sea-stories
interrupted by sea-kisses
tasting of salt.

ACKNOWLEDGEMENTS

I wish to thank Damian Smyth and the Arts Council of Northern Ireland for their support, Offaly County Council and Rosalind Fanning for a week's residency at the Tin Jug Studio in Birr, the Stevenson Society for a month's residency at the Sumburgh Head lighthouse in Shetland, and, for their valuable critical response to work in progress, the members of Word of Mouth and Penelope Shuttle.

'Learning to Whistle' was made into a sculpture by Kevin Killen on permanent display in Down Arts Centre, Downpatrick.

'In a Glass House' is in *On the Grass When I Arrive*, ed. Leo Litvak (Guildhall Press, 2016)

'Ulsterbus Double-Decker, Bog and Swan' is in *Aesthetica Creative Writing Annual 2015*.

'The Pool of Blood' is in *Stony Thursday Book* 14.

'Security', and 'Bread and Jam' are in *Something About Home*, ed. Liam Harte (Geography Publications, 2017).

'Bordering' is in *Washing Windows: Irish Women Write Poetry*, ed. Alan Hayes (Arlen House, 2017).

'Note', 'Passing Number Twenty', 'Where Were You in 1916?' are in *Female Lines*, ed. Linda Anderson and Dawn Sherratt-Bado (New Island, 2017).

'The Other Myrrha' is in *Metamorphic*, ed. Paul Munden and Nessa O'Mahony (Future Publications, 2017).

Versions of some poems have been in *Mslexia, Poetry Ireland Review, Cyphers, HU, Banshee, Four X Four, The South Bank Magazine, Acumen, Wordpool, Poethead, Skylight 47, Boyne Berries, Abridged, North-West Words, Crannog*.

NOTES

At the Bellmouth of the Silent Valley
'P-V-RTY', spelt out by a natural scree formation on Slieve Muck, near Kilkeel, is spoken of locally as a landmark, 'Poverty.'

We Wish to Evoke a Sense of the Authentic
Dziga Vertov made the 1928 documentary, *Man with a Movie Camera*.

A City-Break in Lyon
Guignol is the Mr Punch/Everyman figure in traditional Lyonnais puppet shows.

The Feast of the Epiphany and the Ballast Office Clock
6th January is the last day of Christmas, a Catholic holy day. The Dublin clock provoked James Joyce's literary epiphany.

A Business Meeting at the Slieve Donard Hotel
Roger Casement and Edmund Morel met at this Newcastle hotel in 1904 to make plans for the Congo Reform Association.

An Irishwoman Reads Dodo with Keith Douglas
The *Dodo* novels by E.F. Benson were lent to the poet Keith Douglas (1920–1944) while in hospital in World War II.

The Cold Chain
Irina Ratushinskaya (1954–2017) was a Ukrainian teacher and poet, the author of the USSR prison camp memoir, *Grey is the Colour of Hope* (Hodder and Stoughton, 1988).

The thermal sleeve makers were from the Amsafe factory in Bridport, Dorset.

Gráinne Tobin grew up in Armagh and lives in Newcastle, Co Down. She taught English for many years, in further and adult education and in Shimna Integrated College. Her previous books are *Banjaxed* and *The Nervous Flyer's Companion* (Summer Palace Press).

She was a founder member of the Word of Mouth Poetry Collective, which met for 25 years in the Linen Hall Library in Belfast, and contributed to *Word of Mouth* (Blackstaff Press) which was translated into Russian, and to the Russian-English parallel text anthology of members' translations from five St Petersburg women poets, *When the Neva Rushes Backwards* (Lagan Press). She collaborated in setting up Word of Mouth's archive which is deposited in the Linen Hall Library.

She has won the Segora Poetry competition in France and the Bailieboro Poetry Prize.

Some of her poems are available in the Arts Council of Northern Ireland's online Troubles Archive and in Poetry Ireland's archive.